Be an
ARCHAEOLOGIST

BY MARK HARASYMIW

Gareth Stevens
PUBLISHING

Please visit our website, www.garethstevens.com. For a free color catalog of all our high-quality books, call toll free 1-800-542-2595 or fax 1-877-542-2596.

Library of Congress Cataloging-in-Publication Data

Harasymiw, Mark.
Be an archaeologist / by Mark Harasymiw.
   p. cm. — (Be a scientist!)
Includes index.
ISBN 978-1-4824-1211-6 (pbk.)
ISBN 978-1-4824-1198-0 (6-pack)
ISBN 978-1-4824-1445-5 (library binding)
1. Archaeologists — Juvenile literature. 2. Archaeology — Juvenile literature. I. Harasymiw, Mark. II. Title.
CC107.H37 2015
930.1—d23

First Edition

Published in 2015 by
Gareth Stevens Publishing
111 East 14th Street, Suite 349
New York, NY 10003

Copyright © 2015 Gareth Stevens Publishing

Designer: Katelyn E. Reynolds
Editor: Therese Shea

Photo credits: Cover, p. 1 Zoonar/Thinkstock.com; cover, pp. 1–32 (background texture) Korionov/Shutterstock.com; p. 5 Joe Raedle/Getty Images; p. 7 Viktor Lyagushkin/Flickr Open/Getty Images; p. 9 Kenneth Garrett/National Geographic/Getty Images; p. 11 Mario Savoia/Shutterstock.com; p. 13 Eric Cabanis/AFP/Getty Images; p. 15 Claudio Divizia/Hemera/Thinkstock.com; p. 17 Jeff J. Mitchell/Getty Images; p. 19 Ken Welsh/age fotostock/Getty Images; p. 21 J Boyer/The Image Bank/Getty Images; p. 23 edella/iStock/Thinkstock.com; p. 24 US Navy's Online Library of Selected Images/Wikipedia.com; p. 25 Emory Kristof/National Geographic/Getty Images; p. 26 Time & Life Pictures/Mansell/Getty Images; p. 27 Zbynek Burival/Shutterstock.com.

Printed in the United States of America

CPSIA compliance information: Batch #CS15GS: For further information contact Gareth Stevens, New York, New York at 1-800-542-2595.

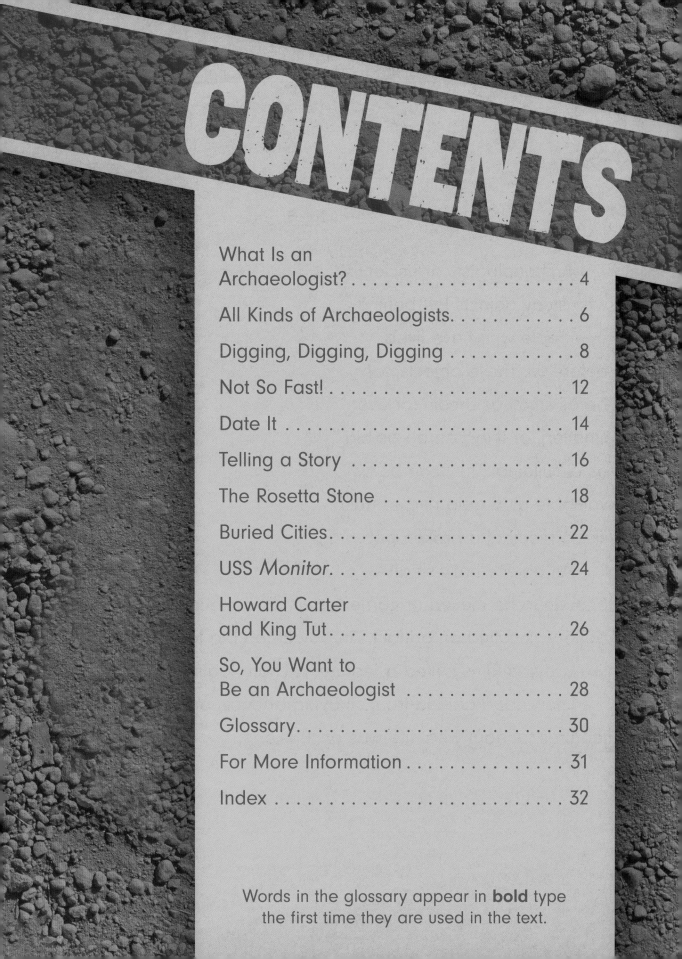

CONTENTS

Words in the glossary appear in **bold** type
the first time they are used in the text.

WHAT IS AN ARCHAEOLOGIST?

Archaeologists are scientists who study objects left behind by people who have lived before us. These objects can be as small as a coin (or even smaller), or they can be as big as a building! They can be as valuable as a gold ring or trash like a piece of a broken pot.

An object that's small enough to be moved or carried, such as a piece of pottery, is called an artifact. An object too big to move, like a pyramid, is called a feature. Archaeologists use the knowledge gained from studying artifacts and features to learn what life was once like.

EXPERTS WHO NEED EXPERTS

Archaeologists work with other types of experts such as metallurgists and conservators. Metallurgists are scientists who study metals and can help archaeologists identify what kinds of metals are in an artifact. Conservators are specialists trained in repairing and caring for objects so they're not damaged by light or air.

You might think of archaeologists digging for artifacts in far-off places. This archaeologist is searching for ancient objects in Miami, Florida! An Indian village may have been located there more than 1,000 years ago.

5

ALL KINDS OF ARCHAEOLOGISTS

Since archaeology is defined as the study of things people have left behind—and people have been on Earth for a very long time—it's usually broken into time periods, regions, or even more focused studies. It's easier for an archaeologist to become an expert on **prehistoric** Indians or underwater archaeology than to become an expert on all peoples, time periods, and places. This way, archaeologists can focus their studies.

So, if you know you're really interested in ancient Greece or Native American battles, you might want to be an archaeologist who concentrates on just that area. However, you'll have to study much more than just these subjects at first.

NOT THE SAME THING

Have you heard of paleontology? It's the study of prehistoric life. However, paleontologists focus on the remains of plants and animals, not humans. They leave ancient humans to the prehistoric archaeologists. Paleontologists may work to find dinosaur bones! This is yet another interesting career in science.

This underwater archaeologist has found the remains of a shipwreck. This is a great career for someone who loves the water and is interested in sea battles.

7

DIGGING, DIGGING, DIGGING

When many people picture archaeologists, they imagine them digging. That's because sand, dust, soil, and mud can build up over artifacts and features over hundreds or even thousands of years. Sometimes entire locations become hidden from view because of natural events, such as floods and **volcanic eruptions**.

In ancient cities, it's often not natural events that cover **sites**, but the people living there! People knock down older houses to build new ones. Roads are laid over older paths. Sometimes, many different structures are built in the same place over hundreds of years. Artifacts of the earlier peoples may be found buried under or around these sites.

DIGGING TOOLS

Archaeologists use many different kinds of tools in their work. You might guess the most common tools of an archaeologist on a dig: shovels, brooms, and brushes. Archaeologists also use **sieves**. These tools are handy to find tiny artifacts that can be missed when digging through lots of dirt and sand.

Archaeologists use hand tools, like brushes, to uncover objects carefully.

9

Did you ever wonder how archaeologists know where to dig? They might match ancient maps to modern maps to find out where to start. They may see odd formations in photographs taken from airplanes or by **satellites**. These may suggest people long ago changed the landscape.

Archaeologists also use tools that send out sound waves or radio waves to find buried objects. These waves of energy travel through the earth and bounce off artifacts or features deep within the ground.

Sometimes finding a dig site is just an accident. People digging holes for other reasons, such as farmers and construction workers, may come across buried artifacts and features.

OOPS!

In 1974, Chinese farmers made an accidental archaeological discovery. While digging a well, they discovered the tomb of the first Chinese emperor (246 BC–210 BC). Within the tomb, archaeologists found thousands of terra-cotta soldiers, horses, and pieces of military gear. This amazing find provided historians with new information about ancient Chinese history.

These soldiers are made of baked reddish clay called terra-cotta. However, they were found with actual swords, spears, and bows in their hands, as if they were ready to attack!

11

NOT SO FAST!

Archaeologists take certain steps before they start an **excavation**. First, they have to receive permission to dig on the land from the landowner or the government. The next step is to make maps of the site and take many photographs before the digging starts. The excavation will change the look of the land, so it's important to record how it looked originally.

Archaeologists divide the dig site into a **grid** to help them remember where artifacts were found. Sometimes archaeologists leave parts of the excavation site untouched. This is so future archaeologists who have better tools can search the site.

THE DIG IS DONE

As the archaeologist completes the excavation, many notes, drawings, and photographs are taken of the surrounding area. Even the soil where artifacts are found is saved to test for chemicals or other matter. Archaeologists are thorough because they never know what information can be learned now or by future scientists.

These archaeologists are carefully recording where they found the artifacts they've uncovered. Early human remains have been found inside this cave in southwestern France.

13

DATE IT

It's not enough to just find ancient objects. Archaeologists have to figure out how old they are. All living things contain **radioactive** carbon, also called carbon-14. Once they die, the carbon starts breaking down at a constant rate. A scientist can learn the age of bone, shell, and wood objects by measuring how much carbon-14 in them has broken down. Carbon dating can identify the age of these things up to 50,000 years old!

There's also a way to date objects made of rocks or **minerals** by measuring different kinds of radioactive matter found in them. Called potassium-argon dating, it can date objects back 2 million years!

THAT WAS EASY!

Some objects are easy to date, especially if the date is found on the object itself. This is called self-dating. This sometimes occurs with items like coins. Knowing the date of an item like a coin can help date an object found right next to it on the dig. That's called relative dating.

15

TELLING A STORY

After the excavation is done and the artifacts are dated, archaeologists then start the next major part of their job: **interpretation**. They use the facts they've gathered and combine them with what other scientists have learned about the people and history of a place. Then, they explain what they think happened at the site and why they think the findings may be important.

This interpretation is really just a good guess about what happened. It's a lot like piecing together a story without knowing all the facts. Many objects were probably destroyed before an archaeologist could study the site.

PUBLICATION

Once an archaeologist decides on an interpretation, the findings are published so they're available to both scientists and others in the community. Other archaeologists are interested in the findings so they can use the information in their own work. Publication also allows people who aren't scientists to learn what archaeologists have found out about human history.

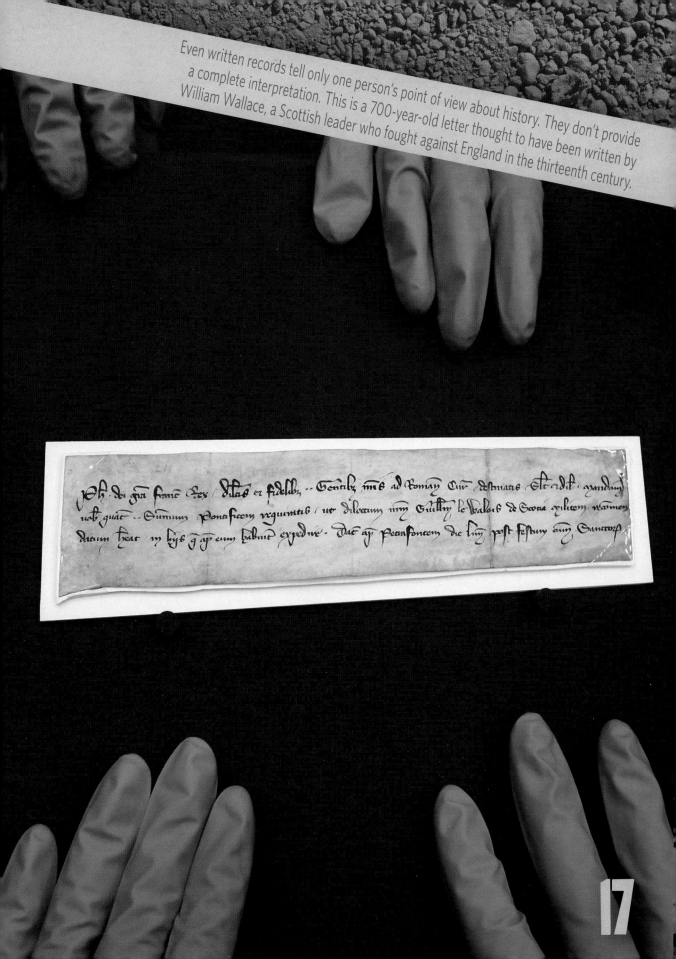

Even written records tell only one person's point of view about history. They don't provide a complete interpretation. This is a 700-year-old letter thought to have been written by William Wallace, a Scottish leader who fought against England in the thirteenth century.

THE ROSETTA STONE

An important find occurred in 1799 in Egypt that sparked millions of people's interest in archaeology. Soldiers from France discovered a stone with writing on it as they were tearing down a wall in the town of Rosetta.

The stone was dated March 27 in the year 196 BC. It featured three different kinds of writing: ancient Greek, **demotic script**, and hieroglyphics, an ancient Egyptian writing system that used symbols and pictures. Several copies of the writing were made, and **scholars** from different countries raced to be the first to figure out its meaning. By 1802, the Greek and demotic sections were translated.

DEMOTIC DETECTIVES

Ancient Greek was known to some at the time of the discovery of the Rosetta Stone. Scholars noticed that the demotic script was similar to other ancient languages that they knew. By using clues based on that understanding, the demotic section of the tablet was soon fully translated.

You can visit what is now called the Rosetta Stone at the British Museum in London, England.

When ancient Egypt was taken over by other nations and peoples, the knowledge of how to read their hieroglyphic writing slowly died out. The Rosetta Stone provided the key to understanding it. Experts realized that the same message was written in Greek, demotic, and hieroglyphics. They didn't know what each hieroglyph meant, however.

One scholar, Jean-François Champollion, was able to crack the code in 1822 by identifying certain words in the hieroglyphic section that corresponded with the same words in the Greek and demotic sections. By building on that knowledge, Champollion was soon able to translate the whole hieroglyphic section.

ANCIENT EGYPT UNLOCKED

Cracking the code of the Rosetta Stone meant that hieroglyphs on Egyptian artifacts could now be read. Hieroglyphic writing in ancient Egyptian buildings, tombs, temples, and scrolls could now be understood. The study of the artifacts of ancient Egypt became very popular, and many archaeologists began to focus on the study of ancient Egypt, called Egyptology.

The message on the Rosetta Stone was written by Egyptian priests. They stated that their ruler, called the pharaoh, was a respectful worshipper of the Egyptian gods. This is a giant version of the stone.

21

BURIED CITIES

On August 24 in the year AD 79, Mount Vesuvius erupted in what is today Italy. The Roman cities of Pompeii and Herculaneum were buried by feet of ash and rock, and more than 2,000 people died. No one could live there for many years after, and, over time, people forgot about the cities—until 1738, when archaeological excavations began.

Archaeologists found many items undisturbed since the eruption, such as ovens containing loaves of bread and jars holding fruit. They even uncovered the skeletons of people who died. About one third of Pompeii still remains buried under volcanic ash, so there's much more exploring and studying to be done.

FROZEN IN TIME

The ruins of Pompeii and Herculaneum are important because they provide a "snapshot" of ancient Roman cities. Other ancient cities, like Rome itself, have had people living in them for thousands of years, rebuilding structures and making it hard to have a complete and clear picture of what life was like.

Archaeologists filled hollow spaces in the volcanic layers near Pompeii and Herculaneum with plaster to re-create bodies, such as the one shown here.

USS MONITOR

Not all archaeological work involves searching for ancient artifacts and features. In 1974, an important archaeological find from the American Civil War (1861–1865) was found off the coast of Cape Hatteras, North Carolina.

In 1862, the USS *Monitor*—a ship used by the North's Union navy—began flooding during a terrible storm. Officers called the USS *Rhode Island* to tow

The USS Monitor floated very low in the water. This made it hard to hit with cannon fire, but it took on water easily during storms.

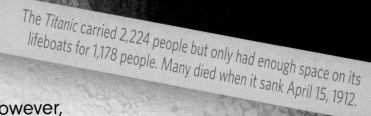

The *Titanic* carried 2,224 people but only had enough space on its lifeboats for 1,178 people. Many died when it sank April 15, 1912.

the ship to safety. However, the *Monitor* took in too much water and sank. After reading the *Rhode Island*'s records, a team of scientists, including an underwater archaeologist, were able to locate the *Monitor*. During the search, the scientists came across the wrecks of 22 other ships!

TITANIC

Robert Ballard found the wreck of the RMS *Titanic* in 1985. This paved the way for future underwater archaeologists to visit the ship's remains in the Atlantic Ocean, about 13,000 feet (3,962 m) under the surface. Since 1985, more than 5,000 artifacts have been brought up. Scientists are even thinking about raising the ship itself!

HOWARD CARTER
AND KING TUT

Howard Carter was a British archaeologist who found the tombs of many ancient Egyptian pharaohs. In 1922, Carter made his most famous discovery in Egypt's Valley of the Kings: the tomb of King Tutankhamun, popularly called King Tut. It had been spared the fate of other Egyptian tombs. Robbers hadn't broken in and stolen the tomb's riches.

A CURSE?

Twelve people who had been present at the opening of Tutankhamun's tomb died within 7 years. These deaths started a rumor that there was a "mummy's curse" on the people who entered the tomb. Carter didn't believe in the curse, however. The archaeologist died 16 years later.

Famous archaeologist Howard Carter is shown here examining Tutankhamun's coffin.

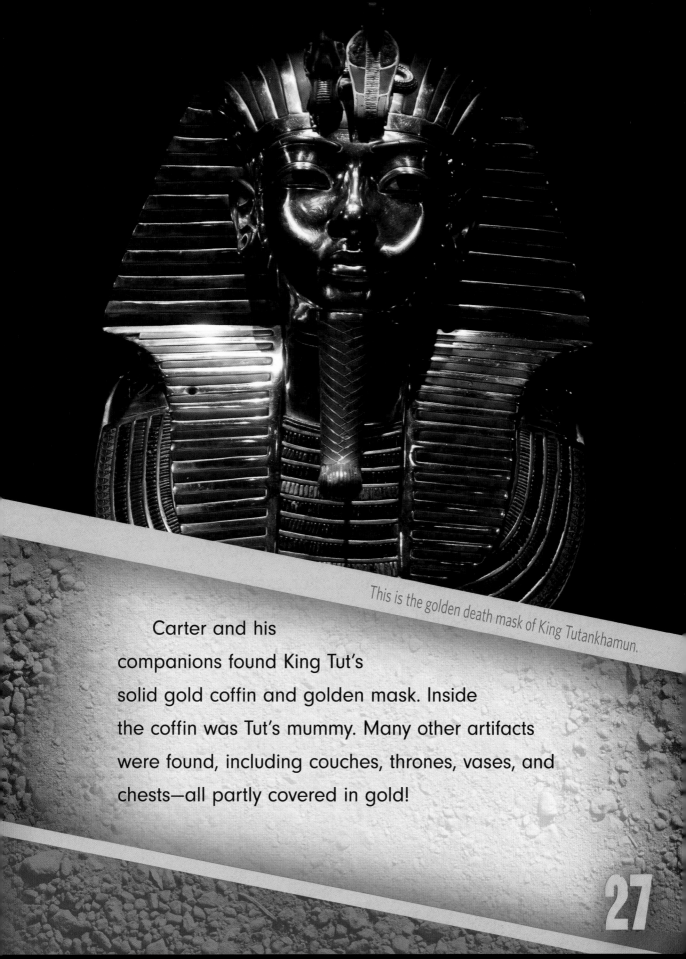

This is the golden death mask of King Tutankhamun.

Carter and his companions found King Tut's solid gold coffin and golden mask. Inside the coffin was Tut's mummy. Many other artifacts were found, including couches, thrones, vases, and chests—all partly covered in gold!

SO, YOU WANT TO BE AN ARCHAEOLOGIST

You can prepare yourself now to become an archaeologist. History, science, English, and math are all important classes for a future archaeologist. In college, students interested in archaeology usually major in anthropology, which is the study of humans. Some schools have an archaeology lab or a museum that offers training or work opportunities. Mastering a foreign language is also useful. For example, an Egyptologist would find it helpful to speak and understand Arabic to talk to modern-day Egyptians. Being able to read the writings of ancient Egyptians would be necessary as well.

Archaeologists also need excellent study, reading, and writing skills. Keep learning all you can about famous discoveries. The next one might be yours!

NOT JUST DIGGING

Not all archaeologists travel around the globe searching for places to dig. Some protect important sites that have already been excavated. Others work in museums or teach at colleges. Whatever your talents, archaeology probably has a special job for you.

TIMELINE OF ARCHAEOLOGICAL DISCOVERIES

1738 Excavation begins of the Roman town of Herculaneum.

1748 Excavation begins of the Roman town of Pompeii.

1799 The Rosetta Stone is found in Egypt.

1822 Jean-François Champollion translates the Rosetta Stone hieroglyphs.

1922 Howard Carter discovers Tutankhamun's tomb.

1974 The USS Monitor is found off the coast of North Carolina.

1974 The tomb of China's first emperor is discovered.

1985 The Titanic is found in the North Atlantic Ocean.

GLOSSARY

demotic script: a simple form of hieroglyphics used in ancient Egypt

excavation: the act or process of digging and removing earth in order to find something

grid: a set of squares formed by crisscrossing lines

interpretation: an explanation of the meaning of something

mineral: matter in the ground that forms rocks

prehistoric: having to do with the time before written history

radioactive: putting out harmful energy in the form of tiny particles

satellite: an object that circles Earth in order to collect and send information or aid in communication

scholar: someone who has a great deal of knowledge about a subject

sieve: a tool used to separate large bits of matter from smaller bits of matter or solids from liquids

site: a place where something happened

volcanic eruption: the bursting forth of hot, liquid rock from within the earth

FOR MORE INFORMATION

BOOKS

Adams, Simon. *Archaeology Detectives.* Hauppauge, NY: Barrons Educational Series, 2009.

Farndon, John. *100 Things You Should Know About Archaeology.* Broomall, PA: Mason Crest Publishers, 2011.

Steele, Kathryn. *Stones and Bones: Archaeology in Action.* New York, NY: PowerKids Press, 2013.

WEBSITES

Archaeology
education.nationalgeographic.com/education/ encyclopedia/archaeology/?ar_a=1
Read about several different excavations.

How Archaeology Works
science.howstuffworks.com/environmental/earth/ geology/archaeology.htm
Learn how the study of archaeology developed and more about what an archaeologist does.

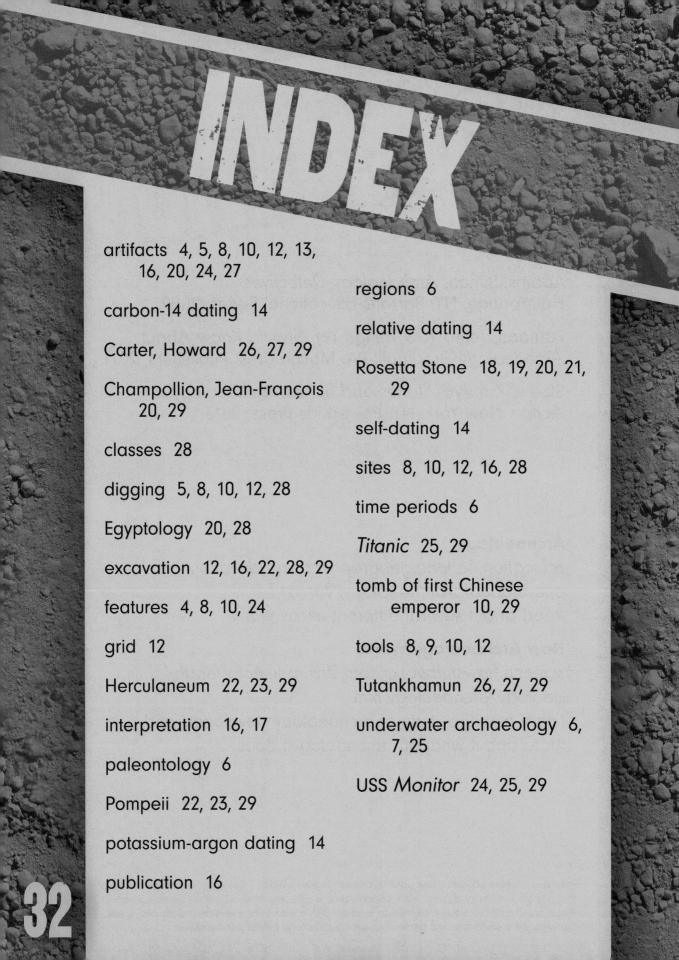

INDEX